Taking Stock:
Community Policing in Chicago

Wesley G. Skogan, Lynn Steiner, Jill DuBois,
J. Erik Gudell, and Aimee Fagan

Institute for Policy Research
Northwestern University

July 2002
NCJ 189909

Sarah V. Hart
Director

This program was supported under award number 94–IJ–CX–0046 by the National Institute of Justice, with funds transferred from the Office of Community Oriented Policing Services, U.S. Department of Justice.

Findings and conclusions of the research reported here are those of the authors and do not reflect the official position or policies of the U.S. Department of Justice.

The National Institute of Justice is a component of the Office of Justice Programs, which also includes the Bureau of Justice Assistance, the Bureau of Justice Statistics, the Office of Juvenile Justice and Delinquency Prevention, and the Office for Victims of Crime.

Contents

Summary 1

Implementing Key Features of Chicago's Program 3
    Problem solving. 4
    Turf orientation. 4
    Community involvement 7
    Linkage to city services 13
    New tools for police 15

CAPS' Impact on Neighborhood Life 17
    Perceptions of police service 17
    Exploring the relationship between community policing and
        trends in recorded crime. 20
    Neighborhood problems 24

Remaining Challenges 28
    Energizing program implementation 28
    Continued immigration. 29
    Resource allocation 30
    Finances 30
    Leadership transition. 31

Suggested Reading 31

Notes 32

Summary

Chicago's community policing program began in April 1993 with the announcement of the Chicago Alternative Policing Strategy (CAPS). After a developmental period in several police districts, CAPS expanded in spring 1995 to involve the department's entire patrol division. The program has continued to evolve; some elements were dropped or altered radically, and others have been put into place. The program celebrated its sixth anniversary as a citywide initiative in spring 2001, which provided an occasion for taking stock of its accomplishments.

Throughout its existence, CAPS has been evaluated by a team from Northwestern University. Supported by grants from the National Institute of Justice, State agencies, and private foundations, they have surveyed police officers and city residents, observed meetings and interviewed participants, analyzed crime trends and demographic data, and monitored program implementation.

The varying degrees of success of many of the program's features offer valuable insight into launching and maintaining a community policing initiative. From the outset, CAPS involved new responsibilities for police. Officers were trained in the problem-solving model—a change from the reactive, traditional responses employed prior to CAPS—and organized around small police beats. They benefited from a host of new tools designed to drive problem-solving and tactical operations. Improved access to city service agencies provided officers with support from resources outside the department. This mobilization of service delivery was highly beneficial in helping police respond to problems of public concern, most notably graffiti and abandoned cars.

CAPS was moderately successful at community involvement. A commitment to turf orientation familiarized officers with neighborhood residents and persistent problems. Police-resident interaction was further facilitated through beat meetings and district advisory committees (DACs). At beat meetings, civilians voiced their concerns so that public opinion could be factored into setting police priorities. The DACs attempted to foster cooperation between residents and police through such activities as marches, prayer vigils, petition drives, and citywide rallies.

CAPS also changed residents' perceptions of police. By the end of the decade, the majority of Chicagoans rated police positively on three measures: demeanor, responsiveness, and performance. The gains, however, still left room for improvement. CAPS had hoped to narrow the gap in perceptions among whites, blacks, and Latinos that existed in the early years of the program. Yet although each group's perceptions of police performance generally grew more positive, the gap between whites and others did not change markedly by 2001.

Recorded crime rates decreased overall throughout the evaluation, and more specifically, whites, blacks, and Latinos all experienced declines in crime. Both robbery and gun-related offenses were down more than 50 percent between 1991 and 1999. The extent to which such declines can be attributed to CAPS is unknown, but an earlier community policing experiment in Chicago found that CAPS was effective at reducing crime. Taken as a whole, a broad range of neighborhood problems declined, but the results varied among racial groups. The bulk of improvement was registered by blacks, and whites reported smaller gains. Latinos, on the other hand, perceived that conditions in their neighborhoods were deteriorating, and by the end of the 1990s, were the most likely group to rank selected measures of crime and social disorder as big problems.

Although overall trends are promising, challenges remain:

- CAPS has not benefited all of Chicago's diverse population. Despite a marketing campaign targeted at Spanish-speaking Latinos, integrating the city's Latino residents into the program has been difficult. Latinos report worsening conditions and have not experienced the declines in various crime categories reported by other groups. This situation is magnified by the fast growth of Chicago's Latino population; Latinos are projected to move past whites and become the second largest population group in the city by 2005.

- By and large, beat meetings are successful but fail to produce consistently noticeable results. DACs, on the other hand, struggle to create a meaningful role for themselves (i.e., a role different from that of beat meetings). Part of the problem is that DACs tend to underrepresent the communities they support, particularly Latinos, and rarely fulfill advisory responsibilities.

- Support for CAPS by police managers and officers has fluctuated. After opening with great anticipation, the program went stagnant and lacked true direction. Beginning in 1999, however, CAPS personnel ushered in new initiatives in an attempt to revitalize the program. The results of these efforts are yet to be realized.

Over the years, the CAPS evaluation has focused on program implementation issues and on the effects of program implementation on the quality of life in Chicago. This report describes the program and details some of the changes that have taken place in the city's neighborhoods during the course of the evaluation. It identifies the challenges that CAPS continues to face and describes new initiatives that were launched by the city as community policing entered the new millennium. The report is directed to criminal justice practitioners and community residents who want to know about the changes that took place in America's big cities during the 1990s, the founding era of community policing.

Implementing Key Features of Chicago's Program

CAPS is an ambitious program, and it is beyond the scope of this report to describe all of its elements or the findings of the evaluation. (More details about CAPS can be found in the readings listed at the end of this report.) This section examines five key features of Chicago's community policing initiative and describes how these features work. Data are drawn from observations of beat meetings and surveys of participants, interviews with activists, police department crime files and activity reports, surveys of police officers and city residents, and city agency databases.

Problem solving

A problem-solving model forms the heart of Chicago's community policing initiative. In CAPS, officers are expected to move beyond responding in traditional fashion to individual calls and instead adopt a proactive, prevention-oriented stance toward a range of neighborhood problems.

Chicago's problem-solving model defines problems as chronic concentrations of related incidents. These incidents are linked mostly by common locations, but also by common victims, offenders, or methods of operation. The persistence of problems may point to a common set of causes, and dealing with these underlying causes can prevent future problems. In keeping with these premises, Chicago adopted a five-step model to guide the problem-solving efforts of police and residents:

- Identify and prioritize problems.
- Analyze problems.
- Design response strategies.
- Implement response strategies.
- Assess the success of response strategies.

Because this kind of systematic thinking about chronic conditions was alien to a city accustomed to reactive policing driven by 911 calls, it was necessary to train both police and neighborhood residents on how to implement the model. From 1995 to 1997, most patrol officers and more than 10,000 residents were taught to analyze how offenders and victims collide at particular locations to create crime hot spots.

Turf orientation

To solve problems using the methods of community policing, Chicago's police patrols had to become more acclimated to the communities in which they worked. This was accomplished by organizing patrol work into 279 police beats, 270 of which were residential. Nine or 10 officers were assigned to each beat, and a sergeant was named to oversee them and lead quarterly team meetings that involved officers from all shifts. Maintaining turf orientation brought new challenges to the departments and individual officers:

- Officers were supposed to stay in one place long enough to develop partnerships with and trust among community residents.

- The community focus meant that officers needed to spend more time working with the community and less time answering radio dispatches.

- In order to give careful attention to residents and to neighborhood-specific problems, officers were required to know their beats—including hot spots, crime trends, and community resources.

Keeping beat units in place was central to turf orientation but was difficult because Chicago responds to a high percentage of 911 calls. A management study revealed that the department had to hire more police to respond to dispatches while keeping officers on their assigned beats. For several years, the department's antiquated 911 and radio system made it difficult to ensure that beat teams were dispatched to calls within their beat, and useful information about this was difficult to assemble. Field sergeants were supposed to intervene on the radio to correct misassignments and encourage officers to "step down" from the radio to work on problems, but few did so. The assignment-bidding process limited managers' ability to keep officers on long-term assignments. The department's union contract specified how officers were assigned to districts and watches, and those with enough seniority could switch assignments. In addition, temporary assignments, vacations, relief duties, and compensatory time off also made it difficult to maintain staffing stability and keep the same officers appearing at monthly beat meetings.

Eventually, the dispatching process was adjusted to keep officers on their assigned beats while answering calls. In dispatching teams, priority was given to categories of calls in which beat officers' knowledge of local conditions could make a difference. Some of the burden of responding to 911 calls shifted to free-roving rapid-response units. Tactical teams, youth officers, and detectives were expected to work more closely in support of beat officers and more readily exchange information with them and the community. Updated computer technology also aided turf orientation.

By 1998, this aspect of the program was fairly successful. The department's initial goal was to keep beat teams on their turf for 70 percent of their dispatches; in 1998 they hit an average of 66 percent. Reaching the target proved easiest to accomplish in high-activity beats. Exhibit 1 plots the relationship between the average monthly volume of dispatches on each of the city's 279 beats and two measures of beat integrity—team integrity and call integrity.[1] Unit integrity rose with dispatch volume, meaning the department was best able to keep its new beat teams in place where they could keep busy locally and not be sent elsewhere. On the other hand, beat teams could not keep abreast of events in high-activity areas. When residents in these areas called, they were *less* likely to be served by a beat unit because beat team officers were very busy. Thus, the percentage of calls receiving a response by the beat team was lowest there, and free-roving rapid-response units had to pick up the slack. Overall, call integrity averaged only 35

Exhibit 1: Dispatch Volume and Two Measures of Beat Integrity

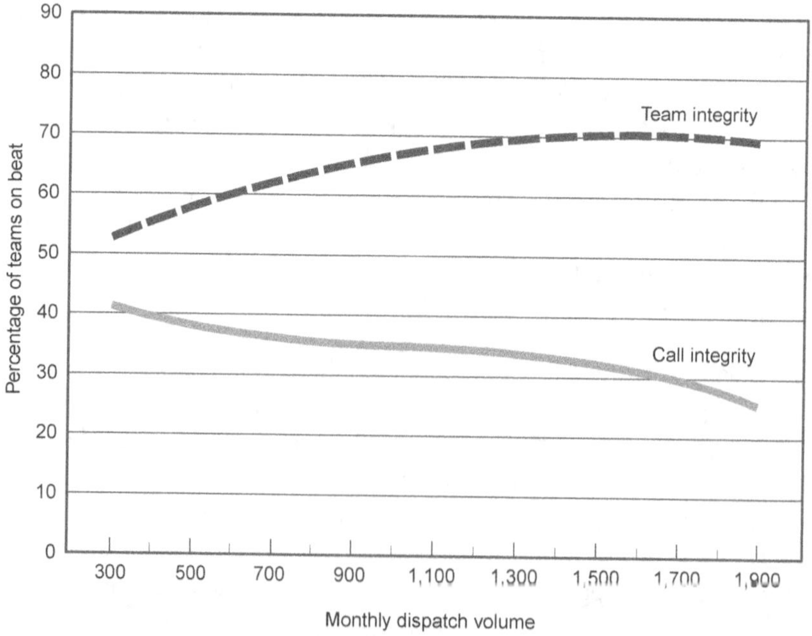

percent because in many areas the beat teams were overloaded with work, and one two-officer team per shift could not do the job.

Aspects of the program that were designed to focus officers on solving problems within their beats were less successful. Beat officers were supposed to have time free from responding to calls so they could work with community members and develop problem-solving projects. However, in a special survey of more than 1,000 officers who attended beat meetings, only 30 percent of beat officers indicated they often had time for preventive work rather than reacting to radio dispatches. Fewer still said they could request and be granted downtime to work on beat problems. Less than one-third reported that their sergeants frequently intervened on the radio to keep their dispatch priorities intact. Officers working the critical 4 p.m.-to-midnight shift were found to be in the best position to become involved with the community, because residents were at home and beat meetings were held in the early evening hours. However, officers on this shift were also the busiest and least likely to have the time to do so.

Community involvement

When viewing neighborhood problems, the public often focuses on threatening and fear-provoking *conditions* rather than discrete and legally defined *incidents*. They concern themselves with casual social disorder and the physical decay of their community rather than with traditionally defined serious crimes. The police, however, are organized to respond to the latter—even earlier surveys in Chicago found that few officers were interested in dealing with noncrime problems. Therefore, CAPS reorganized police to enhance communication and consultation among them and neighborhood residents. This also was advantageous to police in setting priorities.

As officers involved in neighborhood work quickly learn, many residents are deeply concerned about problems that previously did not get serious police attention. Effective community policing requires responsiveness to citizen input concerning the needs of the community, and it creates new roles for residents to become involved in securing safe neighborhoods. One option has been to train residents in problem solving, which is one of the program's key features. Chicago also has instituted beat meetings and DACs to facilitate community involvement.

Beat meetings. Beat meetings provide an important link between residents and police who work in their neighborhood. They began citywide in 1995 and are held in such places as church basements and park buildings all over the city. During the 1990s, approximately 250 beat meetings were held each month. The meetings serve as a forum for exchanging information and prioritizing and analyzing local problems. They allow police and residents to get acquainted with each other and provide an opportunity for residents to organize their own problem-solving efforts. The meetings frequently feature presentations by detectives or police from special units. Representatives of city service agencies, aldermanic staff, school personnel, local business owners and landlords, and organizers from area community groups also make appearances.

During the 1990s, an average of seven police officers attended each beat meeting, including the beat sergeant, the beat officers on duty, and a few beat team members from other shifts. To encourage attendance by the latter, they are paid overtime at a yearly cost of nearly $1 million. Exhibit 2 charts monthly meeting attendance and the cumulative total attendance at 16,606 regular beat meetings from 1995 to 2000. In 1997, about 5,400 people citywide attended beat meetings each month; in 1998, that figure rose to about 5,800; and in 1999, approximately 5,600 people attended. As illustrated, attendance varies by season. It is historically low in December and January and peaks in July or September. In December 2000, attendance hit an all-time low (1,838) as near-record cold and snow gripped Chicago. Through the end of 2000, nearly 390,000 Chicagoans attended beat meetings.

Because the city's police beats vary widely in size (the boundaries were drawn more than a decade ago to equalize police workloads), attendance rates that take the adult population into account shed the most light on variations in involvement from area to area. When combining these rates with crime and demographic information about the beats and the results of citywide surveys and studies of meeting participants, the evaluation found that—

Exhibit 2: Trends in Beat Meeting Attendance, 1995–2000

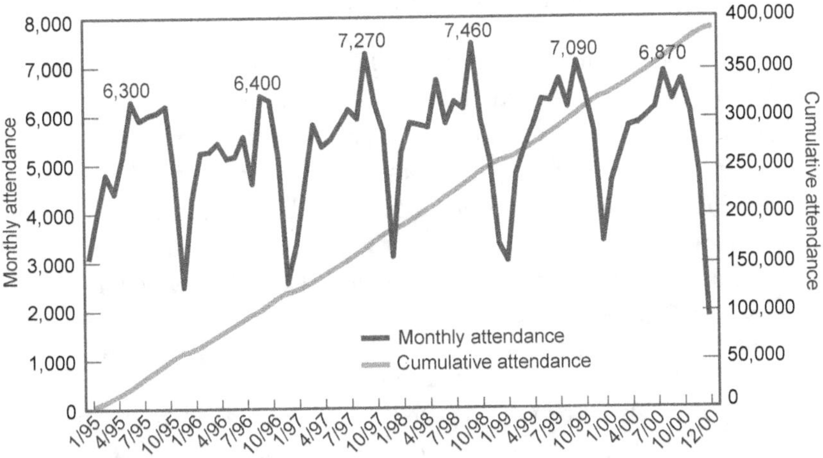

Note: Includes estimates for meetings held but data missing.

- More than 60 percent of Chicagoans knew about beat meetings, and approximately 14 percent reported attending at least one meeting per year. Television was the most common source of information about CAPS, but it did not appear to stimulate involvement. Personal contacts, local fliers and signs, stories in neighborhood newspapers, recruitment efforts by police, and block clubs that worked on behalf of the program sparked attendance.

- Attendance rates were highest in predominantly black beats and lowest in white areas. Attendance was highest among Latinos in areas where the Latino percentage of the population exceeded 60 percent. These meetings usually involved translators and an ample supply of Spanish-language materials.

- The local violent crime rate was the strongest statistical correlate of beat meeting attendance. Such property crimes as burglary or car theft were only weakly linked to area attendance rates, but vandalism was strongly related to meeting participation.

- Attendance at beat meetings was strongest where other institutions were weak. A larger proportion of residents turned out in beats where measures of school performance and achievement were low and where residents reported serious health problems.

- Older, homeowning, long-term residents attended more often than their counterparts, and the number of frequent attendees within an area determined cumulative meeting attendance. Regular attendees were pleased with what went on in the meetings: They thought meetings helped find solutions to neighborhood problems, they saw changes taking place as a result of the meetings, and they were more optimistic than occasional attendees about the quality of police service in the area.

- Participants got involved in their own problem-solving projects. Approximately 75 percent reported working on problems in their area, and 35 percent involved other people they met at beat meetings in their efforts. The strongest determinants of involvement in problem solving by beat meeting participants were networking (e.g., seeing each other at meetings or talking on the phone), frequency of beat meeting attendance, and block-club membership.

- Beat meetings were good for disseminating information and promoting a sense of community involvement, but often did not provide an effective venue for creative problem solving by residents or police. Most meetings were run efficiently and featured the distribution of crime maps and other information. Civilians played a role in conducting approximately two-thirds of the meetings; those were the best run. Although residents always brought up problems, many meetings did not discuss solutions; when they did, solutions were proposed most often by police. Beat meetings were supposed to provide accountability, but police reported back on their efforts only about 60 percent of the time, and residents described what they had done only about one-third of the time. Most efforts described by police at these meetings were traditional (e.g., driving by the scene more frequently and ordering potential troublemakers to "move on"). Participants rarely left beat meetings with an assigned task or committed to a specific postmeeting activity.

Although beat meetings were conducted regularly throughout the city, the evaluation found some shortcomings. Many meetings strayed from their role in prioritizing and acting on problems and focused too much on complaints by residents about personal concerns and demands that police fix problems for them. Ultimately, few beat meetings led to much citizen involvement or problem solving. In response, the police department is offering more training sessions for patrol officers, sergeants, and the civilian "beat facilitators" that help plan and lead the meetings. Teams of civilian trainers who were usually stationed at the police training academy are beginning to attend meetings and work with participants in beats where police deemed the sessions unproductive. A small city agency was created and hired about 45 community organizers who focus on increasing resident attendance at the meetings and supporting problem-solving projects. Nevertheless, beat meetings have been helpful in creating a direct and energetic relationship between residents and police. The evaluation recommends finding ways to coordinate the efforts of contiguous beats that share common problems and problem-solving capabilities.

District advisory committees. DACs seek to develop joint police-citizen projects and are seen as a vehicle to advise police commanders in each of the city's 25 police districts. DACs are composed of community leaders, school council members, ministers, business operators, and representatives of significant organizations and institutions in the district.

Since the beginning of CAPS, however, DACs have struggled to create a meaningful role for themselves. Formally, they are charged with helping police identify and prioritize crime and disorder problems in their communities; assisting in the planning of district problem-solving strategies; and working to mobilize residents around district problem-solving projects, including such collective activities as marches, petition drives, and citywide rallies. In practice, few DACs follow through on all of their responsibilities.

Five years after their formation, the role of DACs in planning and priority setting still has not jelled. This failure may be attributable as much to the police department's formal planning process as to the DACs' inability to carve out a strong role in identifying and prioritizing problems in strategic ways. In comparison with beat meetings, DACs have never engaged in strategic thinking about identifying and allocating resources to address chronic problems of concern to wide segments of their districts. Too many members have remained focused on particular concerns, often to the detriment of the meetings. Police commanders have rarely involved their DAC chairs in planning efforts that extend beyond the agenda for the next meeting. DACs also have not recognized the importance of assessing and critiquing police efforts and identifying those that seem to speak effectively to community concerns. Beyond hearing their commander "read the crime statistics," they have received little information about police operations.

Furthermore, DACs have not been very successful in representing all segments of their communities. Most DACs should be diverse in composition, because police districts are large and their boundaries often encompass disparate groups that vary by race, class, and lifestyle. DACs noticeably underrepresent the city's large Latino population, and smaller but rapidly growing immigrant groups (particularly Asians) are invisible at this level. DACs do not independently represent residents' views, and they typically find it difficult to attract and retain members, which raises concern about their viability.

The evaluation found that in most districts, the police set the agenda for DAC meetings, controlled all information about police operations, supervised the efforts of active subcommittees, and approved—if not actually initiated—significant DAC activities. Rather than being able to press the community's interests, their anomalous position is clear: As appointed creatures of the police department, DACs have limited capacity to act independently or to voice an agenda substantially counter to that of their "advisee." They receive more advice than they give.

Despite these deficiencies, DACs can point to a few solid accomplishments. They provide vocal residents with a venue for assuming insider roles in community policing that they find personally rewarding. More significantly, many DACs foster subcommittees that effectively tackle specific district issues, ranging from domestic violence to problems of senior citizens. Each DAC is required to have a court advocacy group that identifies locally important cases and presses judges and prosecutors to review them with care. These advocacy groups have been the most universally effective activity sponsored by DACs, but their success can be attributed more to the training, staff support, resources, and guidance provided to them directly by city workers than to their grassroots character.

Linkage to city services

If police open themselves to public input but respond to community concerns with remarks such as "that's not a police matter," no one will want to become involved. To avoid such a situation, the city has addressed issues of public concern as part of its commitment to overall crime prevention. A department publication notes that—

> CAPS recognizes that graffiti, abandoned vehicles and build-
> ings, malfunctioning street lights and other signs of neighbor-
> hood disorder do have an adverse effect on both crime and the
> public's fear of crime. By addressing these relatively minor
> problems early on, police and other government agencies can
> prevent them from becoming more serious and widespread
> crime problems.[2]

Community policing inevitably involves an expansion of the police mandate to include a range of concerns previously outside their com-
petence. Solutions to concerns voiced by neighborhood residents with their beat officers frequently require the assistance of other city agencies.

Mobilizing services for problem solving. Chicago always envisioned that the delivery of city services would be an integral part of the CAPS program, but making it work was difficult. An interagency task force worked on the logistics of coordinating agency efforts against problems. Programmers developed a software system that logged in, tracked, and recorded the final disposition of police service requests and gener-
ated user-friendly reports that could be double checked in the field. District commanders and agency troubleshooters met to iron out interagency communication problems. Changes were made in city ordinances to expedite building demolitions and car tows, and civilian coordinators saw to it that CAPS' problem-solving projects had the service support they required.

During the program's developmental period, the service delivery component was one of the most successful elements of CAPS. The evaluation found that in contrast to matched comparison areas, physical decay decreased in the worst-off prototype areas, and several experimental districts made effective use of the service-delivery process to target such problems as abandoned buildings, trash, and graffiti.

City services address graffiti and abandoned-car problems. A 1998 citywide survey found that half of Chicagoans thought graffiti was either some problem or a big problem in their neighborhood, and 32 percent expressed similar concerns about abandoned cars. Residents who turned out for beat meetings that same year were more emphatic about these two problems: 76 percent thought graffiti was a problem in their neighborhood, and 59 percent were concerned about abandoned cars.

To determine how effective the city was at targeting services in response to these concerns, a "service need" measure was created by combining responses to citywide surveys conducted from 1996 to 1998. About 8,000 city residents were interviewed in those surveys, enough that there were at least 10 responses from 220 of the city's 270 residential police beats. Responses to questions about neighborhood problems were averaged to estimate the extent of graffiti and abandoned-car problems in each beat. City databanks contributed indicators of the distribution of relevant service responses for 1997 and 1998. During those 2 years, there were nearly 180,000 graffiti site cleanups and 83,000 car tows. The data revealed that the average beat was cleaned 646 times, and 225 cars were towed. Because beats vary greatly in size, rates of service per 10,000 residents were calculated using updated estimates of the population for each beat. Exhibit 3 illustrates the relationship between these need measures and service delivery rates.

The link between need for and delivery of these two services was substantial. Both graffiti cleanup and car tow rates rose with public demand, although they leveled off in areas that expressed the greatest concern. Statistically, other factors correlated with service delivery, but need measures predominated. Land-use factors influenced graffiti cleanup rates, including the proportion of commercial and manufacturing properties to residential properties in each beat.

Exhibit 3: Beat Needs and Service Delivery

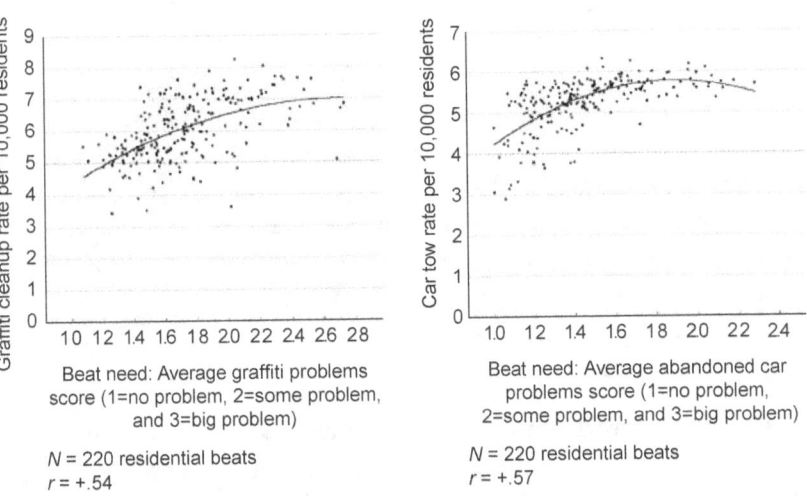

Beat need: Average graffiti problems score (1=no problem, 2=some problem, and 3=big problem)

N = 220 residential beats
r = +.54

Beat need: Average abandoned car problems score (1=no problem, 2=some problem, and 3=big problem)

N = 220 residential beats
r = +.57

Business establishments were not represented in the residential survey, but they had problems too. Graffiti cleanups were more frequent in heavily populated Latino and immigrant areas, in densely populated beats, and among concentrations of older buildings. Controlling for the survey measure of need, car tows were more frequent in older areas, lower income beats, and Latino and black communities.

Citizen involvement seems to have played a role in steering service delivery. In both examples, service delivery rates were higher—controlling for need and other factors—where beat meeting attendance was high. During 1998, the evaluation surveyed more than 5,200 beat meeting participants about their concerns. In meetings where residents expressed great concern about a particular problem, services also addressed it more frequently than otherwise would be expected.

New tools for police

In addition to improved access to the standard menu of agency services, Chicago developed a number of new tools for addressing chronic problems.

Crime analysis. Crime analysis is a key component of community policing in Chicago because it is used to provide the knowledge base driving both problem-solving and traditional tactical operations. An easy-to-use crime-mapping system was developed that runs on personal computers at each district station, using data that are updated constantly via a network. Crime maps and offense data are distributed routinely at beat meetings and are accessible to the public at each police station. New procedures were developed to encourage information sharing among officers across watches about events on the beat. Furthermore, the city's dispatching system was upgraded to support community policing and was linked to a 311 number for nonemergency service requests.

Task force enforcement of housing ordinances. The city created a roving task force that enforces antigang and drughouse ordinances. The team includes police and building, health, and fire inspectors. The task force can bring both criminal and civil cases against building owners who refuse to negotiate or comply with an abatement plan that brings their buildings under control and up to code. In some instances, jurisdiction of such cases has been removed from regular courts. For example, building cases and civil charges arising from health code violations and rules regulating gang and drug houses are placed in a new administrative hearing unit. This unit processes cases swiftly and facilitates case settlement through mutually agreed-on steps to remediate underlying problems. Landlords frequently agree to improve their buildings, enhance security measures, screen and evict bad tenants, and attend beat meetings in return for an abeyance of some or all of their often-hefty fine. An extensive program also was developed to assist landlords in screening and evicting tenants.

Cooperation with city legal staff. Prosecutors also have become involved in CAPS. The county attorney, who handles serious criminal cases, opened storefront offices to work with residents on offenses of interest to the community. These offices assist the police with complex or recurring problems, prosecute all hate crimes, and conduct seminars and education projects promoting crime prevention. The city's law department, which has more expertise in civil cases, also has stationed attorneys in selected district headquarters. Here they work directly with beat officers on problem buildings and on gang and drughouse abatement projects.

CAPS' Impact on Neighborhood Life

Aside from analyzing implementation issues, the CAPS evaluation also sought to determine the effects of the program on society. Would a switch from traditional to community-centered policing change how police were perceived by the community? Would CAPS be perceived differently across Chicago's racially diverse neighborhoods? Would CAPS affect crime rates? Would neighborhood problems improve and, if so, who would benefit?

Perceptions of police service

One goal of CAPS was to increase popular confidence in the effectiveness of police. Some of the best evidence of residents' perceptions comes from the first 2 years of the evaluation, when areas of the city still being served by traditional policing could be compared with districts experimenting with CAPS. This phase of the evaluation found that perceptions of police responsiveness improved in four of the five experimental districts (and not at all in three of the four comparison areas), and that it improved among whites and blacks but not Latinos. Perceptions of police effectiveness and demeanor also improved in the two predominantly black experimental districts but not in their comparison areas.

To examine what happened when the program grew to encompass the entire city, the evaluation conducted annual citywide public opinion surveys. Responses to questions about fairness, politeness, helpfulness, and personal concern shown by police were combined to form a police *demeanor* index. Questions about how effective the police were at preventing crime, helping victims, and maintaining order were combined into a *task performance* index. Police *responsiveness* was measured by questions about how well they dealt with problems that concerned residents, worked with residents to solve problems, and responded to community priorities.

Exhibit 4 illustrates trends in these measures from 1993 to 2001. It charts the percentage of respondents who gave police a positive average rating on each index. Even at the outset, most Chicagoans believed they were treated well by police, which did not leave much room for improvement. In 1993, police averaged a positive score on the police demeanor index from two-thirds of survey respondents; that figure peaked at 75 percent in 1999. Driving the increase in the demeanor index was the percentage of respondents who thought police were helpful to residents, which rose from 84 to 90 percent over the period. Indexes rating police responsiveness and performance showed more notable gains. The responsiveness index rose about 15 percentage points. The largest increase resulted from the percentage of respondents who thought police were doing a good job working with residents to solve problems, which rose from 38 to 52 percent over the period. The task performance index rose 11 points, from 37 to 48 percent. In this category, new police efforts to prevent crime were rated most favorably, rising from 41 to 58 percent.

These findings represent solid gains in favorable perceptions of police. The dashed line highlighting the 50-percent mark in exhibit 4 emphasizes that the perceptions of a majority of Chicagoans moved into the positive range on two of three measures. But the 50-percent mark also emphasizes that ample room exists for improvement. After more than

Exhibit 4: Trends in Assessments of Police Service Quality

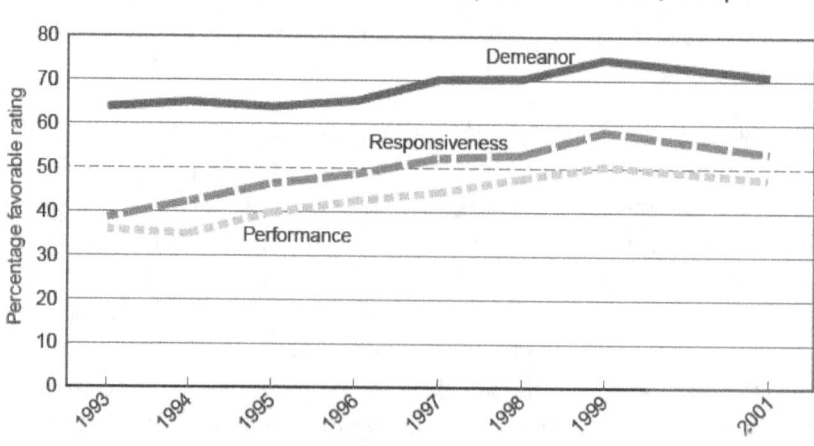

Note: No survey data were collected in 2000.

7 years of community policing, just under half of the public thought that police were doing a good job at preventing crime, helping victims, and maintaining order, while less than 55 percent thought they were doing a good job responding to community concerns. During the 1990s, "the glass" went from being "less than half full" to "a little more than half full."

Perceptions of police by race. Another important goal of CAPS was to mend the breach between police and Chicago's large minority communities. In the early years of the program, blacks and Latinos were 2.5 to 3 times more likely than whites to report that the police were unfair, impolite, unconcerned, and unhelpful. This dissatisfaction was expected to make CAPS a tough sell in many neighborhoods.

Exhibit 5 combines the three measures of police service quality (from exhibit 4) into a single index and presents by race the percentage of respondents who each year gave police a positive average rating on the survey.[3] Exhibit 5 illustrates the across-the-board improvements in residents' views of the quality of police service. Police approval ratings rose from 51 to 61 percent among whites, from 24 to 40 percent among blacks, and from 31 to 46 percent among Latinos. Although overall views improved, these percentages indicate that the gulf

Exhibit 5: Assessments of Police Service Quality by Racial/Ethnic Groups

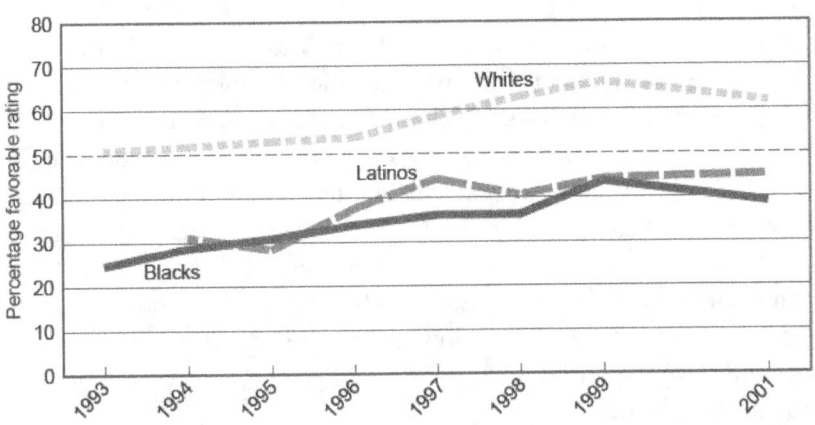

Note: No survey data regarding quality of service by police were collected from Latinos in 1993 or from all racial/ethnic groups in 2000.

between whites and others was nearly as great in 2001 (15 to 20 percentage points) as it was in 1993. In the aggregate, less than half of blacks and Latinos still approved of police performance.

Perceptions in other cities. Another way to consider Chicagoans' views of the police is to compare them with the views of residents in other cities. In 1998 the Bureau of Justice Statistics surveyed residents of 12 large and mid-sized cities about their views of the quality of service and community-oriented programs by police serving their neighborhoods.[4] In this survey, even after years of experience with community policing, residents of Chicago still ranked their police near the very bottom on important measures. Chicago scored second worst in terms of overall satisfaction with the quality of police services. Only 16 percent of the city's residents reported they were "very satisfied" with police who served their neighborhood, while in most cities that figure was above 20 percent and peaked at 31 percent. In the 12-city survey, the gap between white and black residents of Chicago (20 percentage points) also was second largest. The survey found that awareness of community policing and participation in anticrime meetings were the highest in Chicago, but they did not directly translate into satisfaction with how well police were doing their job.

Exploring the relationship between community policing and trends in recorded crime

Any decline in crime is welcome news, and the magnitude of the decline that has occurred in some U.S. cities during the past decade has been unexpected news as well.[5] Researchers and practitioners have puzzled over crime patterns and argued over where credit should be given. Chicago is no exception. Many categories of crime peaked in 1991 and have since been in decline. The rate of decline in Chicago has lagged behind that in some cities but is ahead of others. Rates of some crimes have declined citywide, while others have gone down only in selected communities. In Chicago, as in many cities, the decline began before community policing programs were even on the drawing board.

Exhibit 6 depicts trends in Chicago for most standard crimes (exclud-
ing high-volume property thefts and low-volume arson). The largest
decline documented in exhibit 6 is for robbery, which was down 56 percent in Chicago between 1991 and 2000. Robbery has long been con-
sidered a bellwether urban crime, combining weapon use, risk to life
and limb, and premeditated and predatory intent. A related indicator—
the percentage of all offenses involving a gun—was down by 55 percent
during the same period (not presented in exhibit 6).[6] Auto theft, an
offense that is fairly accurately reported by victims and recorded by
police, was down by 37 percent. Murder and rape, the least frequent of
the offenses depicted, declined 32 percent and 44 percent, respectively.
(Murder and rape are graphed on a separate scale in exhibit 6 so that
trends are visible.) Burglary—the highest volume offense depicted—
decreased 46 percent. A smaller decline was registered in the rate of
aggravated assault and battery, which was down 37 percent. Assault is
an extremely heterogeneous and difficult-to-interpret crime category
that includes (among other things) domestic violence, gang battles, bar
brawls, violence in schools, and disputes between neighbors.

Trends in recorded crime by race. In most categories, the largest
declines have occurred in the highest crime parts of the city. Exhibit 7
presents selected trends for beats that have been grouped by racial

Exhibit 6: Trends in Recorded Crime

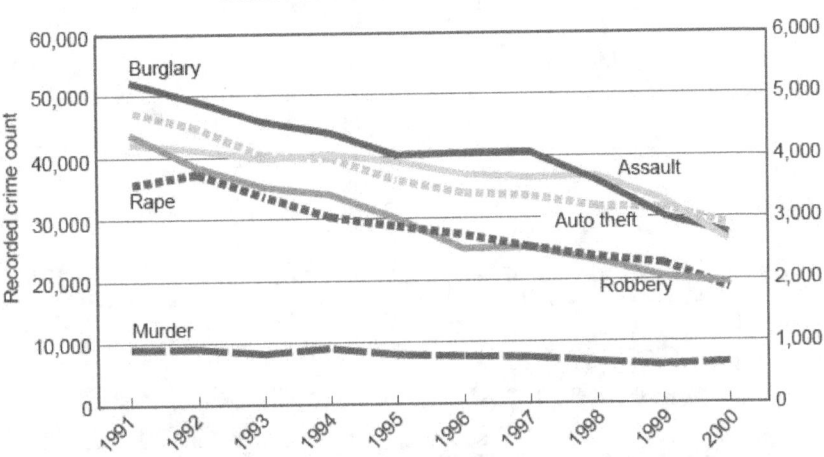

Note: Murder and rape data are scaled to the right axis.

composition. The city's 270 residential police beats were divided into
71 predominantly white areas, 121 heavily populated black areas, 32
areas where Latinos account for an average of 60 percent of the population, and 46 diverse areas. Because the groups differed in size, exhibit
7 presents rates of crime per 100,000 residents in each group. In general, as well as in the examples shown in exhibit 7, crime rates decreased
in all areas but most dramatically in black communities. Crime rates
generally declined the least in predominantly white areas, where rates
were low originally.

Exhibit 7 presents trends only for offenses that are significant for their
volume and relative accuracy of reporting. From 1991 to 2000, the

Exhibit 7: Trends in Recorded Crime Among Racial/Ethnic Groups

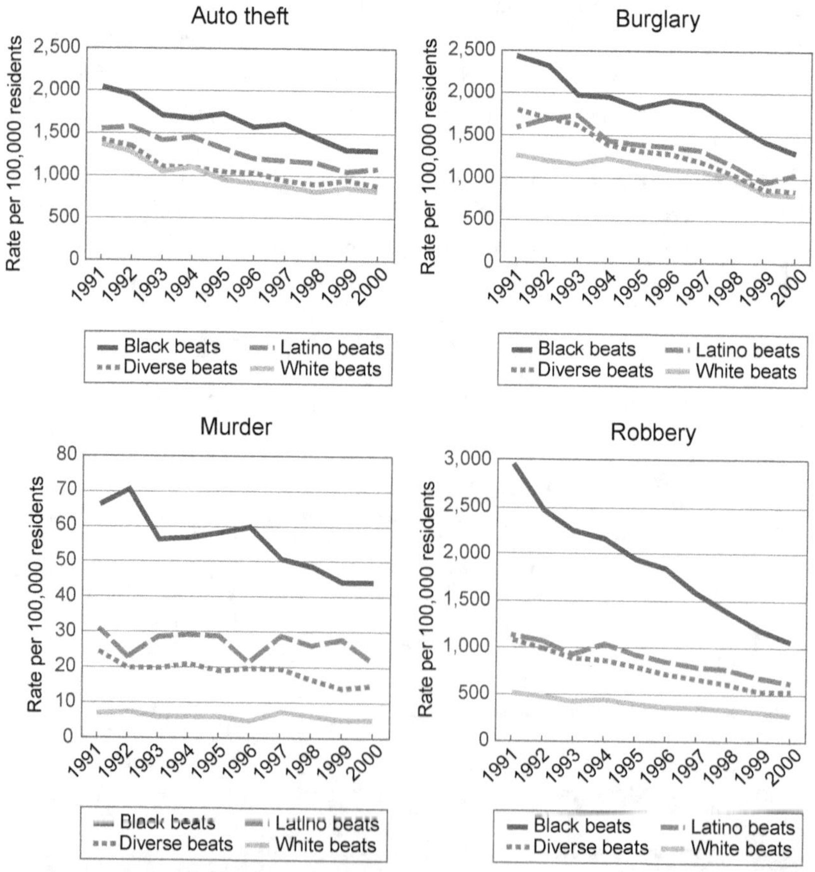

large decreases in crime registered by residents of predominantly black beats were apparent: Robbery was down by 60 percent (from 2,918 to 1,166 incidents per 100,000), burglary by 49 percent, murder by 33 percent, and auto theft by 33 percent. Crime also declined in predominantly white beats. The murder rate there dropped even though it was so low in 1991 that it had little room to fall (from 6 to 5 incidents per 100,000, or only 11 percent of the rate in black areas). Crime rates in heavily populated Latino areas declined less dramatically and typically fell somewhere between rates observed in black and white beats.

CAPS' role in declines in recorded crime rates. Can these declines be attributed to Chicago's community policing program and the thousands of officers hired in support of it? The answer is not clear because the decline in crime began before the introduction of CAPS, and significant numbers of officers did not appear until 1996. However, as evidenced by the impact of CAPS in the original prototype districts and a set of matched comparison areas, the evaluation indicated that the program did reduce crime in those districts, including burglary and auto theft in one district, street crime in another, and gang and drug problems in two other districts.

Other factors influencing drops in recorded rates. As data from the 1990 census grow more outdated, it becomes difficult to gauge trends of many other important factors influencing crime, including immigration and suburban flight, the strength of families, income inequality, and even the number of people living in the city. Although Chicago has shared in the Nation's improving economy, the decline in the city's crime began during a recession. Incarceration rates are at an all-time high in Illinois, and they certainly play an important role. Gun seizures by the Chicago Police Department, which have long been among the highest in the country, decreased during the period, which is consistent with declining gun use and (perhaps) availability. Prominent criminologists have suggested that declining rates of crime during the mid-1990s might have been the result of maturing drug markets,[7] which possibly reduced the level of drug-related violence and weapon use. Drug-related homicides have declined more quickly than homicides overall in Chicago. Research in other cities has found that homicide rates rise and fall with indicators of the extent of crack cocaine use. Urinalyses of arrestees in Chicago point to a modest decline in cocaine use since early 1994 and to a larger decline in opiate use since late 1993.

Although adult violence has been dropping for more than 15 years, one of the most important forces influencing the crime rate is the proportion of young males in the population. According to James Fox, a nationwide decline in the youth population, which reached its lowest point in 1995, may be a potential explanation for the decreasing crime rate in Chicago.[8] However, the Chicago Planning Department estimates a tiny *increase* in the city's youth population (3,507 more youths ages 15 to 24) from 1990 to 1995, so changes in the population of young males cannot explain the drop in crime that Chicago experienced during the 1990s.

Neighborhood problems

In addition to using police crime figures, the evaluation team also tracked trends in neighborhood problems by asking residents about concerns in yearly surveys. Exhibit 8 summarizes survey reports of the perceived magnitude of 13 problems[9] combined into 4 general categories: crime, drugs and gangs, physical decay, and social disorder. It presents the percentage of respondents who thought the issues in each cluster were a problem in their neighborhood. In general, problem measures declined by approximately 7 percentage points from 1994 to 1999, then rose by 4–5 percentage points by 2001.

Two closely intertwined concerns—street drug sales and gang violence—took first place in the 1994 ratings and held that position through the remainder of the study, despite a slight drop (3 percentage points) in concern by 2001. The social disorder category combined reports about gang loitering, public drinking, and disruption in and around schools. Overall, concern about social disorder declined by less than 2 percentage points between 1995 and 2001. The crime index was based on questions about burglary, street crime, car theft, and car vandalism. In 1994, almost 40 percent of Chicagoans thought that crime was a problem; by 2001, that number declined to 35 percent. The physical decay index combined questions about graffiti, junk and

Exhibit 8: Trends in Neighborhood Problems

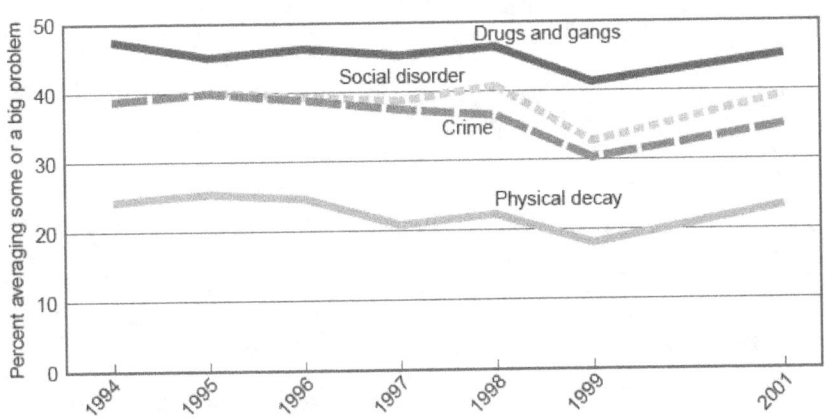

Note: No survey data were collected for the social disorder category in 1994 or for all categories in 2000.

trash, and abandoned buildings and cars. It declined by 2 percentage points. Overall, the biggest declines were gang violence in the drugs and gangs category, school disruption in the social disorder category, burglary in the crime category, and graffiti in the physical decay category. None of these declines, however, was very large.

Neighborhood problems by race. The citywide averages presented in exhibit 8 were not impressive, and on closer inspection, scarcely anyone was average. Exhibit 9 illustrates trends in neighborhood problems by race, using the same topology of neighborhood problems as exhibit 8. It separately tabulates the percentage of respondents reporting that the problems in a cluster constituted close to a "big problem" (the most severe rating) in their community. In general, whites perceived few problems *before* CAPS was announced and by the end of the decade reported only small gains. Because whites were the second largest population group in Chicago, this set a significant upper limit on measures of overall improvement for the city.

The story for the city's blacks and Latinos was much different. They reported about the same level of neighborhood problems in 1994, but by 2001 their experiences diverged dramatically. Ratings for many problems in the black community began high, then dropped

Exhibit 9: Trends in Neighborhood Problems Among Racial/Ethnic Groups

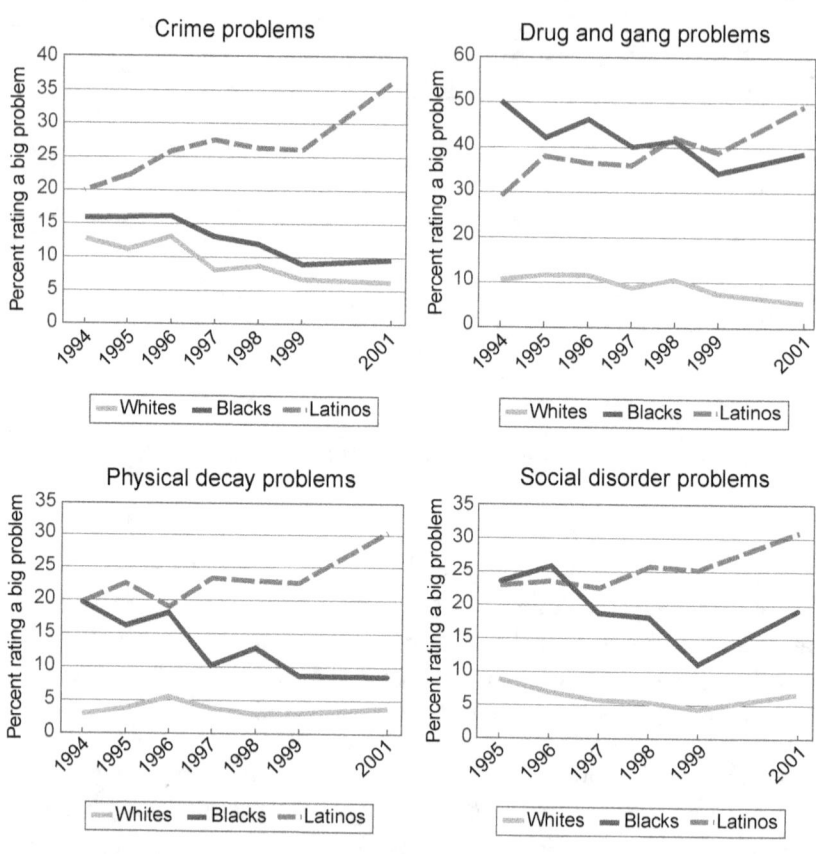

Note: No survey data were collected for the social disorder category in 1994 or for all categories in 2000.

noticeably. In accord with the data on trends in recorded crime, the crime problem ratings offered by blacks dropped by 40 percent from 1994 to 2001. All components of the crime problem index dropped by one-third to one-half for blacks. Reports of drug and gang problems plummeted among blacks, dropping from 50 to 37 percent during the course of the study and sinking as low as 31 percent in 1999. The measures of physical decay and social disorder tracked a similar course.

The situation for Latinos was different further, as they perceived deteriorating neighborhood conditions in all four categories. From 1994 to

2001, all components of the crime problems index increased among the city's Latinos. The increases were large: concerns about burglary rose from 15 to 36 percent and problems regarding street drug sales increased from 23 to 47 percent. In the social disorder category, Latinos saw none of the declines in school disruption reported by other groups (concern among Latinos increased 8 percentage points), nor did they observe improvements in the physical condition of their neighborhoods.

Interestingly, the perception by Latinos that neighborhood problems increased did not mirror the image painted by officially recorded crime figures for Latino neighborhoods. This discrepancy may be traced to language. Reports by English-speaking Latinos paralleled official statistics, whereas Spanish-speaking Latinos reported worsening conditions on every measure of crime in the survey.

As a result, by 2001 the balance of concern about neighborhood problems shifted dramatically in Chicago: perceived conditions in black neighborhoods improved considerably, whereas those in Latino areas deteriorated. The significance of these diverging trends is reinforced by another trend: Latinos are the only large group in the city that is growing in size, and by 2005 they will be the second largest group in Chicago. Much of this growth is fueled by immigration, which increases the difficulty of finding ways to involve them in city programs.

Chicago has made efforts to involve Latinos more in its community policing effort. The publicity campaign supporting the program features components aimed at Spanish-speaking residents. It includes paid promotional announcements and a police-staffed talk show on Spanish-language radio; booths at festivals held in Latino neighborhoods; and wide distribution of posters, fliers, and newsletters in Spanish. Spanish-speaking community organizers work for the city to generate involvement in beat meetings and problem-solving efforts. The city's emergency communications system is staffed to handle foreign-language calls, and the police department has approximately 800 Spanish-speaking officers. Beat meetings held in predominantly Latino areas are routinely conducted in both English and Spanish, although the translators are nearly always police or resident amateurs and the meetings run at a slow pace. The department's cadet diversity training includes role-playing exercises revolving around language issues. Despite these efforts, the integration of the city's Latino residents into CAPS has been difficult, and will continue to deserve more attention as the Latino population increases.

Remaining Challenges

Energizing program implementation

CAPS was launched with a great deal of anticipation, especially in the community. During the developmental phase, it had the close attention of police and city leaders. The coordination and resources required to expand the initiative to encompass the entire city also kept a spotlight on the program. Within a few years, however, the project stagnated. Important structural changes that had been made to the department and the service delivery process remained in place, but implementation of further change was placed on hold. Key personnel at police headquarters and in the field did not understand the program or were opposed to it, and—more important—a routinized administrative system that could monitor, assess, and manage the program was never put in place. When CAPS could no longer rely on the extraordinary efforts of its founders, the momentum of the early years was lost. Many mandatory meetings were held just to go through the motions; key planning documents were completed in perfunctory fashion and filed away; high-level managers evidenced little interest in how well CAPS was being implemented in the districts. Evaluators in the field found little creative problem solving, perhaps because no one in charge was encouraging or supporting it, and commitment to the program among the department's operational managers—sergeants and lieutenants—was spotty. Their immediate superiors had no role in the program and no interest in crafting one.

By the end of 1999, the department had begun to tackle these issues. A new CAPS Implementation Office was created that was headed by a senior manager with experience in community policing. Staff members spent several months in the field observing operations, dropping in on meetings, and interviewing key sworn and civilian leaders about the effectiveness of the program. They then drafted guidelines addressing a long list of organizational problems, the most important of which clarified who is in charge of and accountable for program implementation. Clear CAPS responsibilities were placed on senior managers who in the past had eluded any. Roles were carved out for watch commanders, who are second to commanders in the district chain of command. For the first time, each district has a CAPS management team leader (a lieutenant) who is responsible for all community policing activities.

Efforts are being made to set priorities and link tactical operations to strategic plans. A new, systematic process was put in place for developing practical district plans to address chronic crime and disorder problems. A "mission board" in each station lists daily the activities that are under way to address priority problems identified in the plan. The boards help district managers allocate resources, track tactical operations, and check off goals that have been achieved. Important management efforts were initiated to revitalize the department's planning and resource allocation procedures. Several rounds of training on how to make all of this work were held for managers in each district.

Continued immigration

Latinos and Asians represent the only growing population groups in Chicago. In fact, the Asian population rate is growing faster than the Latino rate, albeit it from a lower base, which means that the Asian population contingent will not displace blacks, whites, or Latinos for several decades. Future initiatives to enhance Asian involvement in community policing will likely meet the same barriers to success—which involve language, culture, and the legal status of a significant number of new residents—as initiatives directed at Latinos. Some of Chicago's new Asian residents are traditional immigrants, while others are refugees. The former often arrive to a welcoming hand from family members and are more easily assimilated because of their technical skills. The latter tend to arrive from humble origins and face grave personal difficulties adjusting to big-city life. The languages and cultures among the city's new Asians residents are even more diverse than those in the Latino community, which increases the challenges faced by the police as they struggle to involve new communities in policing.

Resource allocation

The tremendous churning of Chicago's population, coupled with differential shifts in levels of crime across neighborhoods in the 1990s, has led to an imbalance in resource allocation. The city has been unwilling to confront this challenge because community policing has become so deeply woven into the fabric of neighborhoods. In less than a decade, communities have gained a sense of ownership of beat boundaries and the officers who work within them. Formerly viewed as obscure police administrative units, beats are now the lines along which many residents define their personal territory and around which organizations mount problem-solving projects. Concerned residents, community activists, and local politicians will demand a role in deciding where new beat lines will fall. The city will have to resolve potentially divisive issues, including whether beat boundaries should be drawn to maximize the homogeneity of the resident population or to ensure their diversity. Administrative calculations will have to clarify how much time and effort beat officers should devote to community interaction and problem solving as opposed to traditional crime fighting. Such decisions will signal the city's commitment to each and hold significant consequences for police department budgets.

Finances

CAPS must prove its mettle in the face of declining city revenues and Federal support for police hiring. Staffing for the CAPS initiative flourished in the mid-1990s as the national economy improved and Federal hiring supplements fueled the department's expansion. In 2002, however, city revenues have begun to shrink dramatically and Federal support for police hiring has slowed. Ultimately, budgets provide the bottom-line measure of a city's commitment to community policing; in that respect, Chicago is no different from other cities.

Leadership transition

The generation of police leaders who formulated and guided CAPS through its developmental stage is now on the verge of retirement. Leadership transition often provides the greatest test of an organization's commitment to any program. Across the country, this transition has not always been smooth for community policing programs because new leaders often want to make their mark with new initiatives. One strength of CAPS has been a commitment to the program at the political level—from the mayor's office to the hundreds of groups of residents who assemble each month in support of it. CAPS has grown to be the city's program, not just the police department's program, and this growth provides strong assurance that CAPS will stay the course in the face of future challenges.

Suggested Reading

Skogan, Wesley G. "Community Policing in Chicago," in *Community Policing*, ed. Geoffrey Alpert and Alex Piquero. Prospect Heights, IL: Waveland Press, 1997: 159–174.

Skogan, Wesley G., and Susan M. Hartnett. *Community Policing, Chicago Style*. New York and London: Oxford University Press, 1997.

Skogan, Wesley G., Lynn Steiner, Jill DuBois, J. Erik Gudell, and Aimee Fagan. *Community Policing and "The New Immigrants": Latinos in Chicago*. NIJ Research Report. Washington, DC: U.S. Department of Justice, National Institute of Justice, July 2002, NCJ 189909.

Skogan, Wesley G., Susan M. Hartnett, Jill DuBois, Jennifer T. Comey, Karla Twedt-Ball, and J. Erik Gudell. *Public Involvement: Community Policing in Chicago*. NIJ Research Report. Washington, DC: U.S. Department of Justice, National Institute of Justice, June 2000, NCJ 179557.

Skogan, Wesley G., Lynn Steiner, Jill DuBois, J. Erik Gudell, Aimee Fagan, Jinha Kim, and Richard Block. *Community Policing in Chicago, Year Seven: An Interim Report*. Chicago: Illinois Criminal Justice

Information Authority, 2000. This report, one of a series, is available free of charge from 120 South Riverside Plaza, Suite 1016, Chicago, IL 60606.

Skogan, Wesley G., Susan M. Hartnett, Jill DuBois, Jennifer T. Comey, Marianne Kaiser, and Justine H. Lovig. *On the Beat: Police and Community Problem Solving*. Boulder, CO: Westview Publishing Co., 1999.

————. *Problem Solving in Practice: Implementing Community Policing in Chicago*. NIJ Research Report. Washington, DC: U.S. Department of Justice, National Institute of Justice, April 2000, NCJ 179556.

Notes

1. For clarity, exhibit 1 omits the hundreds of data points that determine the location of each line.

2. Chicago Police Department. "Fact Sheet: The Role of City Services in the CAPS Problem-Solving Model," 1996.

3. The 1993 city survey was small and conducted only in English, so responses by Latinos are not presented for that year.

4. Smith, Steven K., Greg W. Steadman, Todd D. Minton, and Meg Townsend. *Criminal Victimizations and Perceptions of Community Safety in 12 Cities, 1998*. Washington, DC: U.S. Department of Justice, Bureau of Justice Statistics and Office of Community Oriented Policing Services, May 1999, NCJ 173940.

5. Blumstein, Alfred, and Joel Wallman, eds. *The Crime Drop in America*. New York: Cambridge University Press, 2001.

6. The gun crime measure was developed by scanning recorded incidents since 1991 (a total of about 6.3 million records) for gun involvement, independent of their Uniform Crime Report classifications. This measure was developed by the evaluation team and is not a Federal Bureau of Investigation statistic or an official Chicago Police Department figure.

7. Blumstein and Wallman. *The Crime Drop in America* (see note 5).

8. Fox, James A. "Demographics and U.S. Homicide" in *The Crime Drop in America*, Alfred Blumstein and Joel Wallman, eds. New York: Cambridge University Press, 2001.

9. Respondents were asked to rate whether each was a big problem, some problem, or no problem in their neighborhood. The 1994 survey was the first to include questions about neighborhood problems, but the full range of social disorder questions was not included until 1995.

About the National Institute of Justice

NIJ is the research, development, and evaluation agency of the U.S. Department of Justice and is solely dedicated to researching crime control and justice issues. NIJ provides objective, independent, non-partisan, evidence-based knowledge and tools to meet the challenges of crime and justice, particularly at the State and local levels. NIJ's principal authorities are derived from the Omnibus Crime Control and Safe Streets Act of 1968, as amended (42 U.S.C. §§ 3721–3722).

NIJ's Mission

In partnership with others, NIJ's mission is to prevent and reduce crime, improve law enforcement and the administration of justice, and promote public safety. By applying the disciplines of the social and physical sciences, NIJ—

- **Researches** the nature and impact of crime and delinquency.
- **Develops** applied technologies, standards, and tools for criminal justice practitioners.
- **Evaluates** existing programs and responses to crime.
- **Tests** innovative concepts and program models in the field.
- **Assists** policymakers, program partners, and justice agencies.
- **Disseminates** knowledge to many audiences.

NIJ's Strategic Direction and Program Areas

NIJ is committed to five challenges as part of its strategic plan: 1) **rethinking justice** and the processes that create just communities; 2) **understanding the nexus** between social conditions and crime; 3) **breaking the cycle** of crime by testing research-based interventions; 4) **creating the tools** and technologies that meet the needs of practitioners; and 5) **expanding horizons** through interdisciplinary and international perspectives. In addressing these strategic challenges, the Institute is involved in the following program areas: crime control and prevention, drugs and crime, justice systems and offender behavior, violence and victimization, communications and information technologies, critical incident response, investigative and forensic sciences (including DNA), less-than-lethal technologies, officer protection, education and training technologies, testing and standards, technology assistance to law enforcement and corrections agencies, field testing of promising programs, and international crime control. NIJ communicates its findings through conferences and print and electronic media.

NIJ's Structure

The NIJ Director is appointed by the President and confirmed by the Senate. The NIJ Director establishes the Institute's objectives, guided by the priorities of the Office of Justice Programs, the U.S. Department of Justice, and the needs of the field. NIJ actively solicits the views of criminal justice and other professionals and researchers to inform its search for the knowledge and tools to guide policy and practice.

NIJ has three operating units. The Office of Research and Evaluation manages social science research and evaluation and crime mapping research. The Office of Science and Technology manages technology research and development, standards development, and technology assistance to State and local law enforcement and corrections agencies. The Office of Development and Communications manages field tests of model programs, international research, and knowledge dissemination programs. NIJ is a component of the Office of Justice Programs, which also includes the Bureau of Justice Assistance, the Bureau of Justice Statistics, the Office of Juvenile Justice and Delinquency Prevention, and the Office for Victims of Crime.

To find out more about the National Institute of Justice, please contact:

National Criminal Justice Reference Service
P.O. Box 6000
Rockville, MD 20849–6000
800–851–3420
e-mail: *askncjrs@ncjrs.org*

To obtain an electronic version of this document, access the NIJ Web site
(*http://www.ojp.usdoj.gov/nij*).

If you have questions, call or e-mail NCJRS.

www.ingramcontent.com/pod-product-compliance
Lightning Source LLC
Chambersburg PA
CBHW071343310526
45790CB00018B/1220